THE
A-Z
OF
THE KINGDOM OF HEAVEN

BY
R.S. MURRIN

WITH 26 WATERCOLOUR ILLUSTRATIONS BY THE AUTHOR

THIS BOOK IS DEDICATED TO MY GRANDCHILDREN,
LUKE, TABITHA, EMILY, MOLLIE, GRACE, AND HOPE.
ALSO TO CHARLOTTE HARDING AND TOM GRAHAME,
TWO YOUNG CHILDREN FACING DEBILITATING
ILLNESS WITH COURAGE AND DETERMINATION.

With a Preface by the Right Reverend David Walker,
Bishop of Dudley

ISBN No: 978 0 906165 72 0

First Published January 2010

By the same author: "The Hitch-Hiker's Guide to the Galilee"

THIS BOOK IS AN ORIGINAL WORK
PRIVATELY PRINTED IN WALES IN THE TOWN OF LAMPETER
AT THE UNIVERSITY OF WALES REPROGRAPHIC UNIT
AND PUBLISHED BY THE AUTHOR:

R.S.Murrin
Albion Cottage
Peterchurch
Herefordshire
HR2 0RP
Great Britain

Telephone 01981 550656
Facsimile 01981 550432

50% of the cover price of this book will be donated to the Church in Wales Jubilee Fund,
to assist with the rebuilding of the Shuja'iya Family Health Care Centre in Gaza City.

PREFACE

BY THE RIGHT REVEREND DAVID WALKER, BISHOP OF DUDLEY

A few years ago the National Gallery in London staged an exhibition entitled *Seeing Salvation.* Christian artwork from different centuries and different traditions was brought together under one roof to show how, through a whole variety of visual media, Christian men and women have sought to convey to each other the heart of our shared faith.

That exhibition set me off on a personal journey of discovery. I found, as St. Paul reminded his readers in his letter to Rome, that there is much more to our faith than can ever be put into words. Significant among the landmarks for me on that journey, have been the watercolours of Bob Murrin. And so, it is a delight for me to have been invited to contribute these few words by way of an introduction to Bob's book.

The illustrations in this volume will take you into the joy of God in the richness of His creation; they will open up for you the depth of love of Christ as He journeyed for our sakes to the cross; they will afford you glimpses of the Holy Spirit dwelling within and enriching all of our lives.

Bob's rich use of colour reminds us that now we do (as again St. Paul puts it) see only pale reflections of the true reality of God's Kingdom that surrounds us.

This is not a book simply to be read, but one to be opened again and again, to be gazed at until we absorb the images into our own selves and they become part of the prayer we make to God.

THE A–Z OF
THE KINGDOM OF HEAVEN

BY R.S. MURRIN

ONE OF MY MOST PERSISTENT IDEAS HAS BEEN FOR AN ILLUSTRATED BOOK ABOUT THE KINGDOM OF HEAVEN. THIS BOOK IS DEDICATED TO MY SIX GRANDCHILDREN, AND TO CHARLOTTE HARDING AND TOM GRAHAME. IT WAS ALWAYS INTENDED TO BE A CHILDREN'S BOOK, BUT IT HAS FINALLY ENDED UP AS A PUBLICATION FOR BOTH CHILDREN AND ADULTS. I HAVE DECIDED TO KEEP THE PHRASES SUCH AS "DEAR CHILDREN", OR "DEAR GRANDCHILDREN", IN THE TEXT, AS THIS WAS HOW THE ESSAYS WERE ORIGINALLY CONCEIVED.

THIS PUBLICATION HAS TAKEN A LONG TIME TO COMPLETE, BECAUSE THE ORIGINAL IDEA CAME TO ME AS FAR BACK AS 1987, AND THE WATER COLOUR IMAGES, IN PARTICULAR, HAVE DEMANDED MUCH CARE AND ATTENTION. THE ILLUSTRATIONS ARE ACCOMPANIED BY DESCRIPTIVE ESSAYS AND RELEVANT SCRIPTURES, WHICH HELP TO EXPLAIN WHAT THE PAINTINGS ARE ALL ABOUT. I HAVE TAKEN EACH LETTER OF THE ALPHABET AND FORGED A LINK BETWEEN THE TEACHING OF JESUS ON THE SUBJECT OF THE KINGDOM, AND THE ALPHABETICAL SYMBOL. VERY OCCASIONALLY, I HAVE LEFT THE PARABLES, AND GONE TO ANOTHER PART OF THE BIBLE AS THE SOURCE OF INSPIRATION.

'THE KINGDOM OF HEAVEN' IS, OF COURSE, A SPIRITUAL CONCEPT. JESUS USED COLOURFUL IMAGERY TO STIMULATE THE IMAGINATION OF HIS LISTENERS. WHAT IMAGERY! WHAT A KINGDOM! WHEN ASKED WHAT THE KINGDOM OF HEAVEN WAS LIKE, JESUS REPLIED IN HIGHLY COLOURFUL TERMS. IT WAS LIKE A PEARL OF GREAT PRICE, A FISHING NET, A LAMP ON A STAND, EVEN A LUMP OF YEAST! ALL THESE IMAGES ARE, OF COURSE, A GIFT FOR THE ARTIST, AND A BONUS FOR THE WRITER. IN MANY OF THE PICTURES, I HAVE USED MY IMAGINATION, PURE AND SIMPLE. HOWEVER, THE VILLAGE OF VIRA IN THE FRENCH PYRÉNEES HAS PROVIDED THE INSPIRATION FOR MANY OF THE PAINTINGS, AND I EVEN TRAVELLED FROM PETERCHURCH TO ABERYSTWYTH FOR THE WATERCOLOUR OF THE BOAT AND THE FISHING NET! I KNOW THAT YOU WILL ENJOY TRAWLING THROUGH THIS BOOK, AND I HOPE THAT IT WILL GIVE YOU AS MUCH PLEASURE READING IT AS IT HAS GIVEN ME IN CREATING IT. FINALLY, A SPECIAL THANK YOU TO ANNE WATKINS, LIBRARIAN TO THE RELIGIOUS EXPERIENCE RESEARCH CENTRE AT THE UNIVERSITY OF WALES IN LAMPETER, WITHOUT WHOSE HELP AND ENCOURAGEMENT THIS BOOK WOULD NEVER HAVE BEEN PUBLISHED.

R.S. MURRIN, PETERCHURCH   JANUARY 2010

THE
A – Z
OF
THE KINGDOM OF HEAVEN

CONTENTS: ILLUSTRATIONS ACCOMPANY THE TEXT

A IS FOR ANGEL

SCRIPTURE REFERENCE:
SAINT MATTHEW CHAPTER 25 VERSE 31:
JESUS SAID: "WHEN THE SON OF MAN COMES IN HIS
GLORY, AND ALL THE ANGELS WITH HIM, HE WILL SIT
ON HIS THRONE IN HEAVENLY GLORY." (N.L.T)

DEAR GRANDCHILDREN, I HOPE THAT YOU WILL ENJOY THIS ILLUSTRATED BOOK, WHICH I HAVE WORKED ON FOR SOME TIME, ABOUT THE KINGDOM OF HEAVEN. MY FIRST ILLUSTRATION IS 'A IS FOR ANGEL', AND IF YOU THINK THAT THE ANGEL LOOKS A LITTLE BIT LIKE GRANDMA, THEN THAT IS EITHER A COINCIDENCE, OR SOMETHING MAY HAVE BEEN GOING ON DEEP DOWN IN MY IMAGINATION!

THE THEME IS A WELL KNOWN ONE, THAT OF THE 'GUARDIAN ANGEL' — THE ANGELIC SPIRITUAL PRESENCE WHICH GUARDS THE HUMAN PERSONALITY. MY CERTAINTY WAS THAT THIS PARTICULAR ANGEL WAS DRESSED IN GREEN, AND HAD BEAUTIFULLY COLOURED WINGS. THE FACE, EYES, HAIR, AND HALO WERE THE MOST DIFFICULT TO IMAGINE BECAUSE GRANDDAD COULD NOT SEE THE DETAILS AS HE WOULD HAVE DONE IF HE WERE IN THE PRESENCE OF A REAL PERSON. HE HAD TO USE THE POWERS OF HIS IMAGINATION TO ARRIVE AT THE COLOURFUL ANGELIC PRESENCE WHICH YOU CAN SEE IN THIS WATERCOLOUR, WHICH INCIDENTALLY BEGAN ITS LIFE AS A CRAYON DRAWING.

I HOPE THAT YOU WILL USE YOUR IMAGINATION WHEN YOU USE YOUR COLOURING BOOKS, CRAYONS AND PAINTS. PERHAPS YOU WILL COME UP WITH YOUR OWN VERSIONS OF HEAVENLY ANGELS. JUST TO REMIND YOU, ANGELS ARE CHARACTERISED BY GREATNESS, SWIFTNESS, STRENGTH, BEAUTY, WISDOM AND LOVE. A GOOD DESCRIPTION OF GRANDMA, DON'T YOU THINK? IN TERMS OF THE KINGDOM OF HEAVEN, JESUS TELLS US THAT WHEN HE SITS ON HIS THRONE IN HEAVENLY GLORY, ALL THE ANGELS WILL BE WITH HIM. WHAT A WONDERFUL OCCASION THAT WILL BE!

1

A is for Angel

B is for Banquet

Scripture Reference: Saint Luke Chapter 14 verse 13:

Jesus said:
"But when you give a banquet, invite the poor, the crippled, the lame, the blind, and you will be blessed. Although they cannot repay you, you will be repaid at the resurrection of the righteous." (N.L.T)

My dear Grandchildren, one of the key elements of the 'Kingdom of Heaven' is the Banquet. Jesus frequently used the illustration of the Banquet as a way of explaining the true meaning of the Kingdom of Heaven to His listeners. At the Banquet, the Bride – the Church, meets and celebrates with her beloved Bridegroom – Jesus Christ. The guests are the 'Kingdom People' – the blind, the lame, the terminally ill, all those who suffer. The 'Servants' at the table are those who also love the Bridegroom, but, because they are 'whole', they delight in serving and attending to the guests, the 'Kingdom People'.

The scene in Granddad's painting is the dining room at a Hospice. It is actually based at Kemp House, where Granddad once served as Chaplain. The table is set. At the head of the table, the face of Christ oversees the Banquet. The room is flooded with the light of Christ. His blood streams through, over, and along the banqueting table. It is the River of Life. A guest touches, and receives sustenance from the life-blood. Other guests, illuminated by the light of Christ, find that they are 'not far' from the Kingdom of Heaven.

Staff, volunteers and helpers at the Hospice realise that they do not always need the physical sustenance of a meal, as it is their joy and privilege to serve, and to attend to the needs of the 'Kingdom People'. Transfigured, serene, and experiencing salvation, the guests are drawn into the embrace of a loving Shepherd. The Hospice is at its best, providing sustenance, both physical and spiritual, as the Bridegroom takes His honoured place at the table.

This picture was painted in the year 2000, and was one of the early watercolours prepared for the 'A-Z of the Kingdom of Heaven.' Parts of the picture are based on reality, and parts are, again, taken from the imagination. I hope that you will like the painting, even though it may be hard to understand.

Footnote: A major part of this watercolour is featured on the cover of the C.D: "Sounds of Celebration" featuring Kevin Bowyer playing the organ works of Paul Fisher at Blackburn Cathedral. Lammas Records. LAMM 182D.

B is for Banquet

C is for Christ

(The Christ of Ty-Mawr)

Painted at Ty-Mawr Convent, Monmouth, in April 2002

Scripture Reference: St.John Chapter 11 verses 25-27:

Jesus told Martha: "I am the resurrection and the life. Those who believe in me, even though they die like everyone else, will live again. They are given eternal life for believing in me and will never perish. Do you believe this? "Yes, Lord," she told Him. "I have always believed You are the Messiah, the Son of God, the one who has come into the world from God." (N.L.T.)

My son, Thomas, said to me:

"Dad, none of your watercolours would be complete without the application of your 'Bic' pen!"

The 'Christ of Ty-Mawr' has brought so much pleasure to those who have seen it. I hope that it will bring pleasure to you, dear reader, as you look at this energetic watercolour. You may not know that it was painted not far away from Herefordshire, at a convent in South Wales. Ty-Mawr is a community of Anglican sisters at Lydart, near Monmouth, in Gwent, who exercise a ministry of hospitality, prayer and worship. The nuns often welcome Granddad to the 'Print Room', a quiet artist's studio in the grounds of the convent, where I can paint, write, and think, without fear of interruption or disturbance. Ty-Mawr convent itself is set in an idyllic vale of trees, shrubs and flowers. Under one spreading tree, there hangs a bronze statue of Christ, exposed to the elements, a magnificent crucifixion which I have wanted to paint for many years. In the spring of the year of our Lord 2002, I sat down under the tree, and painted as freely as I have ever done. My late friend and colleague, the Reverend Jesse Hillman, upon seeing the finished painting, asked me:

"Bob, did you paint a shehkinah* rainbow of colours around your portrayal of Christ, on purpose?" My honest answer was, and is, that this was not my original intention. However, I am glad that my resulting work does seem to literally burst with colour and with power.

Thank God for the wonderful gift He has given to us.
May God bless all who gaze upon His Son.

Shehkinah: Hebrew, meaning 'The presence or dwelling of God.'

THE
CHRIST OF
TY-MAWR

The Christ of Ty-Mawr

THE DOVE OF PEACE

Scripture References: Psalm 55 verse 6:
"Oh that I had wings like a dove!
For then would I fly away, and be at rest." (AV)

Saint Luke Chapter 3 verse 22:
"And the Holy Ghost descended in a bodily shape, like a dove,
upon Him. And a voice came from heaven, which said:
Thou art my beloved Son; in Thee I am well pleased." (AV)

My dear children; the image of the dove has fascinated and inspired artists for many hundreds of years. The gentle white dove has become a symbol of purity, holiness, and peace for a wide variety of cultures and religions. Hundreds of years before Jesus walked this earth, people of the Jewish faith often purchased doves in the courts outside the temple, bringing them to the priest as part of their ritual offering. At Jesus' baptism in the River Jordan, we are told that the Holy Spirit hovered above the head of Jesus, in the bodily shape of a dove.

When I first began to show my picture of a dove to various people, the response was nearly always the same: "Oh, that's the Dove of Peace!" And so, I have called this watercolour, 'The Dove of Peace.' After studying various photographs of a dove in flight, I finally arrived at this version, an image of the most spiritually significant bird in the history of creation. Very often, doves appear frightened, tender and fragile. They flap their wings with great energy and alarming noise. Why is it, then, that they are symbols of purity, holiness, and peace? Could it be that the white of their plumage is unmatched by other birds? Could it be that their vulnerability is one of the accepted attributes of holiness? Perhaps the answer is to be found in the story of Noah, who trusted the humble white dove to search out habitable land, and whose trust in God was fully rewarded when the dove returned with a twig from an olive branch in its beak. I trust that my personal interpretation will bring a sense of peace to those who look at this watercolour of a dove.

Footnote: The watercolour painting of 'The Dove of Peace' features on the cover of the paperback book 'The Hitch-Hiker's Guide to the Galilee' by the author.

D is for the Dove of Peace

E is for Eye

Scripture Reference: Saint Matthew Chapter 6 verses 22 - 23

Jesus sat down to teach them: "Your eye is a lamp for your body.
A pure eye lets sunshine into your soul. But an evil eye shuts out the
light and plunges you into darkness. If the light you think you have is
really darkness, how deep that darkness will be!" (N. L. T.)

My dear Grandchildren; I must explain that I did not set out with the
intention of painting the extraordinary image which stands in front of me
today, as I write. I had been painting very early on during our holiday at a
converted barn, 'le Grenier' in June 2003, with no idea what the resulting
image might be. It was quite a shock when, after my first skirmish with the
paint, Grandma said to me:

"Bob, your painting looks like the face of the Devil!"

As I continued to paint, the face of the 'Evil One'; the 'Enemy', featuring so
prominently in Jesus' parables about the Kingdom, became more and more
evident. I also realised that the face appearing in my picture was very like the
face of the sculptured Devil beneath the Holy Water Stoup, in the Church at
Rennes-le-Chateau, near Quillan, not many miles away from Vira. I had
already come across a colour photograph of this frightening sculpture in one
of the illustrated guidebooks to the Pyrénées. The Devil's eye, angrily
prominent in the sculpture at Rennes-Le-Chateau, soon became the focal point
of my watercolour. I worked for several hours at the blue, black, and white
pigmentation of the eye, not realising how dramatic this frightening organ, set
in an ugly face, would become.

My series of paintings, entitled "The A-Z of the Kingdom of Heaven" is
intended to be a beautiful and colourful tribute to the teachings of Jesus on the
subject of the Kingdom. However, it is vitally important for all of us to realise
that the Evil One, whose eye shuts out the light of the Gospel, must feature in
any artistic or literary work about the Kingdom of Heaven, if only to remind
us of those negative elements which can hinder the positive advance of the
Kingdom in our lives. It is our duty, with the help of Jesus, to avoid the deep
darkness of evil, and to look out onto the world with pure eyes. We are told
by Jesus that a pure eye will let sunshine into our souls. Shall we close our
eyelids to things that are seen through evil eyes, and allow our eyes to become
an efficient lamp for our body, so that the true light of Jesus illuminates our
inner lives?

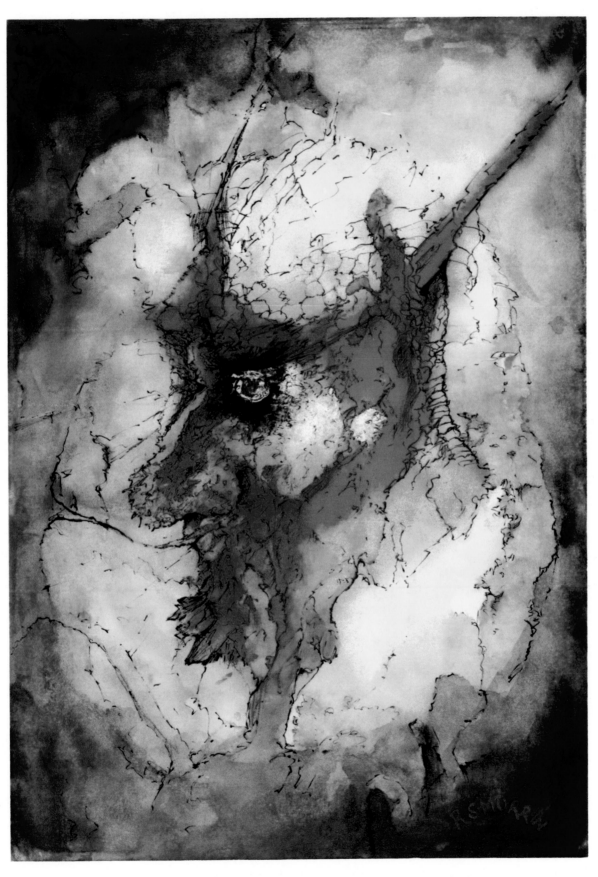

E is for Eye

F is for Fig Tree

Scripture Reference: Saint Luke Chapter 13 verses 6-9:

Then Jesus told this parable: "A man had a fig tree planted in his vineyard, and he went to look for fruit on it, but did not find any. So, he said to the man who took care of the vineyard, 'For three years now I've been coming to look for fruit on this fig tree and haven't found any. Cut it down! Why should it use up the soil?' 'Sir', the man replied, 'leave it alone for one more year, and I'll dig round it and fertilise it. If it bears fruit next year, fine! If not, then cut it down.' (N.L.T.)

Children, the fig tree in my painting, belonging to Monsieur Georges Rouche, in the hilly, sun-drenched village of Vira, in the south eastern Pyrénées, has no trouble producing fruit. When Granddad sat down in late September, 2002, to paint the tree, the branches were wonderfully laden with fruit. Monsieur Rouche had obviously given his tree much time and nourishment in order to encourage the fine harvest of figs which were his earthly reward.

In the Gospel stories, Jesus gives fig trees a hard time. In the Gospel of Matthew, Jesus even curses a fig tree which is not producing a harvest, and, in our extract from Saint Luke's Gospel, Jesus reluctantly gives the fig tree another year to produce fruit. The answer to Jesus' treatment of the fig tree lies in the broader picture of the Kingdom of Heaven. The fig tree is, in fact, an allusion to the nation of Israel, a nation selected for its potential fruitfulness, nurtured by great leaders, and fertilised by the pronouncements of the prophets. The 'Lord of the Harvest' is becoming exasperated with the nation of Israel, the fig tree, because of its reluctance to yield fruit. I am going to end this little essay with a further scripture, from Matthew's Gospel, Chapter 24, verse 32, which I hope you will take to heart:

"Now, learn a lesson from the fig tree."

F is for Fig Tree

G is for Good Samaritan

Scripture Reference: Saint Luke Chapter 10 verse 33:

Then a despised Samaritan came along, and when he saw the man, he felt deep pity. Kneeling beside him, the Samaritan soothed his wounds with medicine and bandaged them. Then he put the man on his own donkey and took him to an inn, where he took care of him." (N.L.T.)

Little children, Granddad's picture of the Good Samaritan was painted one evening at 'le Grenier', a holiday home in Vira, in the French Pyrénées. It is, of course, an imaginative composition, showing the Good Samaritan, kneeling down, attending to the wounded traveller. The powerful rays of the mid-day sun illuminate the landscape, as the Priest and the Levite pass by on the other side, on their way to Jericho. The Samaritan's donkey waits, ears pricked, by a tree, not knowing that his next burden will be the young, badly wounded invalid. The Good Samaritan, although a social outcast, gives his time, his money, his love, and his care to a young Jewish traveller, the victim of an horrific attack. Jesus was always quick to point out that the Kingdom of Heaven was open and available to both Jew and 'outcast'. I love the way the Authorised Version of the Bible concludes the story of the Good Samaritan: Jesus said: "Which now of these three, thinkest thou, was neighbour unto him that fell among thieves?" And he said," He that shewed mercy on him." Then said Jesus unto him,

"Go and do thou likewise."

Good Samaritan

R.S. MURRIL

G is for the Good Samaritan

H is for Harvest (The Tree of Life)

Scripture Reference: Saint Matthew Chapter 9 verses 35-38:
Jesus went through all the towns and villages, teaching in
their synagogues, preaching the good news of the Kingdom
and healing every disease and sickness. When He saw the
crowds, He had compassion on them, because they were
harassed and helpless, like sheep without a shepherd.
Then He said to His disciples: "The harvest is plentiful but
the workers are few. Ask the Lord of the Harvest, therefore,
to send out workers into His harvest field." (N.L.T.)

Dear Grandchildren, if you visit south eastern France in
September, you won't fail to be surprised by the fruitfulness of
the area. The fields of Languedoc Roussilon are, indeed, 'ripe
unto harvest', as one version of the Bible would have it. Grapes,
figs, plums, blackberries, tomatoes, nuts and apples are seen
growing in abundance, often literally hanging from the
hedgerows, inviting those passing by to pick and eat. On one
walking expedition, Grandma and I spotted a magnificent apple
tree, and Granddad made a mental note to return in a day or two
and paint the colourful fruit tree, its apples so obviously ready for
harvesting. Granddad learned later that the name of the apple
tree was: "Reine des Reinettes" (Queen of little Queens), and that
this particular apple tree belonged to a Monsieur Adrian Fabré.
Granddad must have been really inspired by the beautiful apple
tree, because his watercolour is pleasing to the eye, and the
apples are such a lovely shade of red, looking ripe for harvesting,
and even more tempting for 'scrumping'. When Granddad
eventually showed his watercolour to a wider audience, many of
them exclaimed "Oh, that's the Tree of Life!" a title which has
remained with the painting ever since. Children, can you see the
little white butterfly which settled down somewhere, just for a
moment while Granddad was painting the apple tree? And, please
may Granddad leave you with a scripture which might make you
pause for thought? Saint Luke Chapter 6 verses 43 and 45:

"A good tree can't produce bad fruit, and a bad tree can't
produce good fruit. A tree is identified by the kind of fruit it
produces ... A good person produces good deeds from a good
heart."

The Tree of Life
(H is for Harvest)

I.N.R.I.

(Iesu Nazarene Rex Iudarum)
Jesus of Nazareth ~ King of the Jews

Scripture References: Saint John Chapter 19 verses 1-3,
and verses 16-22:

Then Pilate had Jesus flogged with a lead-tipped whip.
The soldiers made a crown of long, sharp thorns and put it
on His head, and they put a royal purple robe on Him.
"Hail, King of the Jews!" they mocked, and they hit Him with
their fists. (N.L.T.)

Then Pilate gave Jesus to them to be crucified. So they took
Jesus and led Him away. Carrying the cross by Himself, Jesus
went to the place called Skull Hill (in Hebrew = Golgotha). There
they crucified Him. There were two others crucified with Him, one
on either side, with Jesus between them. Pilate posted a sign over
Him that read: 'Jesus of Nazareth, the King of the Jews'. The
place where Jesus was crucified was near the city; and the sign
was written in Hebrew, Latin, and Greek, so that many people
could read it. Then the leading priests said to Pilate,

'Change it from "The King of the Jews" to "He said, I am the King
of the Jews."' Pilate replied, "What I have written, I have written.
It stays exactly as it is".

Children, I often wonder whether Jesus' face, at the time of the
crucifixion, was very battered and scarred. We are told that the
soldiers hit Him with their fists! I remember, years ago, watching
a heavyweight boxing match between Muhammad Ali and Brian
London. I think London only lasted two rounds ~ but his face,
and I'll never forget this, looked horribly swollen and bruised,
rather like the face of Jesus in my watercolour painting. Brian
London was a professional boxer; Jesus, however, is God's Son.
How could we humans ever treat Him the way we did, all those
years ago? And, if we don't love him now, today, we continue to
abuse and disfigure His image in us. Surely, He deserves our
unconditional love, now ~ and forever?

I is for I.N.R.I.

J is for Jesus,
Shepherd of the Lost Sheep

Scripture Reference: Saint Luke Chapter 15 verses 3-7:

Jesus said:

"If you had one hundred sheep, and one of them strayed away and was lost in the wilderness, wouldn't you leave the ninety-nine others to go and search for the lost one until you found it? And then you would joyfully carry it home on your shoulders. When you arrived home, you would call together your friends and neighbours to rejoice with you because your lost sheep was found. In the same way, heaven will be happier over one lost sinner who returns to God than over ninety-nine others who are righteous and haven't strayed away!" (N.L.T.)

Dear children; Granddad's painting of Jesus, Shepherd of the lost sheep, is another imaginative composition, using a watercolour technique which was, at the time, quite new to him. In his mind's eye, Grandad had this picture of Jesus, coming down from a hilly area, with the lost sheep on His shoulder. He began the painting by experimentation, with each corner of the paper literally awash with primary colours; red, blue, and yellow. Rushing to the adjoining bedroom, Granddad dried out the surface of the paper with a hair dryer, and, concentrating his gaze on the central area of the paper, he could make out the faintest hint of what he had wanted to create; the figure of Jesus, with the lost sheep on His shoulder. It was now up to Granddad to draw the figure in the centre of the composition, and to complete the surrounding areas, which seemed to be part of some mystical landscape. The final result is a colourful, but dramatic painting, whose subject matter can perhaps be best summed up by another scripture, Saint Matthew Chapter 18 verses 12-14:

"If a shepherd has one hundred sheep, and one wanders away and is lost, what will he do? Won't he leave the ninety-nine others and go out into the hills to search for the lost one? And if he finds it, he will surely rejoice over it more than the ninety-nine who didn't wander away! In the same way, it is not my heavenly Father's will that even one of these little ones should perish."

J is for Jesus

K is for the Kingdom of Heaven

Scripture Reference: Revelation Chapter 5 verses 6 and 13:

Then I saw a Lamb, looking as if it had been slain, standing in
the centre of the throne ... Then I heard every creature in heaven
and on earth and on the sea, and all that is in them, singing:
'To Him who sits on the Throne and to the Lamb, be praise
and honour and glory and power, for ever and ever!' (N.L.T.)

Dear Children; the central theme of this book is the Kingdom of
Heaven. One of the few people to have been afforded a glimpse of
God's heavenly Kingdom during their life on this earth, was Saint
John. His apocalyptic vision, written in the book of Revelation,
was originally thought to be too harrowing for inclusion in the
Bible, and was very nearly omitted. As Granddad began to paint
his own vision of the Kingdom, a line from Shakespeare came
repeatedly into his mind: 'Christ's blood streaming in the
firmament.' The Lamb of God, looking as if it has been slain,
sits in majesty in the centre of the Throne, taking away the sins
of the world. Christ's blood, available for all, swirls continuously
through the universe. Human beings are represented by the
figure at the bottom left of the picture. We are bound tightly by
a snake-like rope of sinfulness which strangles us, forcing us to
stand back from the Kingdom of Heaven, until we are saved by
the Lamb. 'Now', says Saint Paul, 'we see through a glass darkly.'
When salvation comes, we will see clearly.

Chapter 22, verse 1, of the Book of Revelation speaks of the River
of Life: 'Then the angel showed me the river of the water of life,
as clear as crystal, flowing from the Throne of God and of the
Lamb.' In Granddad's picture, the illogical perspective of the
Throne provides a framework for the saving effect of Christ's
blood, and for the healing effect of the River of Life (represented
by the areas of green and blue in the painting). If you find all
these things puzzling, and are thirsty for an explanation;
the Lamb of God, who takes away the sins of the world,
provides an explanation in verses 6 and 7 of chapter 21:

"It is finished! I am the Alpha and the Omega ~ the Beginning
and the End. To all who are thirsty I will give the springs of the
water of life without charge! All who are victorious will inherit all
these blessings, and I will be their God and they will be my
children." (NLT)

K is for the Kingdom of Heaven

L is for Light

Scripture Reference: Saint Matthew Chapter 5 verses 14-16:
Jesus said: "You are the light of the world – like a city on a mountain, glowing in the night for all to see. Don't hide your light under a basket! Instead, put it on a stand and let it shine for all. In the same way, let your good deeds shine out for all to see, so that everyone will praise your heavenly Father." (N.L.T.)

"Kate, I need a lamp!" "What sort of lamp, darling?"
"You know – one of those 'thingy's' with oil inside, and with a wick.
You know, an old-fashioned type of lamp!" "What do you want it for?"
"I want to put it on a stand, and paint it of course!"

Grandma and Granddad looked high and low for a lamp. For several days we looked at every lantern, every street-light, and every candle-stick holder in Fenouillades. Then, to our surprise, we found the very lamp we needed, in an alcove at 'le Grenier', the holiday home rented to us, and belonging to Joy and Bill Greeves. One very bright day, Granddad put Joy's lamp on the brick parapet outside our villa, and began to paint. At the end of the day, all that he had achieved was a very bland painting of a lamp set on a stand. In short, the painting looked dull and lifeless. So, Granddad went to sleep, thoroughly dissatisfied with his work. The following day, Granddad made the early morning cup of tea, just before dawn. The sun was beginning to glint through the trees outside our holiday home, and its rays soon began to burst through the greenery. Suddenly, Granddad thought of a way of bringing his picture of the lamp to life. Could he capture, perhaps; with his watercolours, the sun's rays through the glass of the lamp? Placing the lamp carefully on the parapet – there was thankfully no wind to speak of – Granddad hastily prepared his equipment and began to paint. The light coming towards him through the lamp was almost blinding. As he continued to paint, the dull tones of the previous day became suffused with light. By having enough faith to place Joy's redundant lamp on its stand, Granddad was rewarded with an illustration that will always remain fascinating because of the transforming activity of … 'the light of the world.'

In the Synoptic Gospels; Matthew, Mark, and Luke; Jesus tells us that we are the light of the world. However, in John's gospel, Jesus tells His followers something which Granddad discovered for himself on that sunny morning in the Pyrénées:

"I am the light of the world. Whoever follows me, will never walk in darkness, but will have the light of life." (Saint John Chapter 8 verse 12)

L is for Light

M is for Many Mansions
(The village of Vira, French Pyrénees)

Scripture Reference: Saint John Chapter 14 verses 2-6:

"In my Father's house are many mansions: if it were not so,
I would have told you. I go to prepare a place for you. And if I go and
prepare a place for you, I will come again and receive you unto Myself;
that where I am, there ye may be also. And whither I go ye know,
and the way ye know." Thomas saith unto Him, "Lord, we know not
whither Thou goest; and how can we know the way?"
Jesus saith unto him: "I am the way, the truth, and the life:
no one cometh unto the Father, but by Me." (A.V.)

The village of Vira, set high in the foothills of the 'Pyrénees Orientales',
is the archetypal mediaeval village. I tried to paint this beautiful village in
the late summer of 2002, but ended up with a wishy-washy outline,
failing to capture any relevant detail. The following year, 2003, I tried
again, and ended up with a picture which, I hope, reflects the concept of
a habitation, or village, in which there are 'many mansions'. Walking
through Vira, particularly during the evening, there is nearly always an
eerie silence ~ the houses are built, and prepared for occupation,
but only a few are lived in. Could this be very much like the Kingdom
of Heaven ~ a place where mansions are prepared for us, but, to which,
we are not sure of the way?

For several months, I was not sure of the way forward with this
painting. In actual fact, the detail was not completed while sitting in the
open air, in front of the subject. What happened was that, I sat, one very
quiet night, in our holiday home, and found that my hand was strangely
guided. I seemed to know, intuitively, every stone, every brick, every tile,
every detail of Vira and its surrounding countryside; as if these were
stored in some remote part of my memory. Even the bushes, the trees,
and the fields, seemed to find their own position, shape, and colour
within the composition. They say: "A thing of beauty is a joy forever".
Children, enjoy Vira's many mansions, but remember, that by following
Jesus as the way, the truth, and the life, you will then allow God the
Father to prepare your eventual spiritual home.

M is for Many Mansions

N is for Net

Scripture Reference: Saint Matthew Chapter 13 verses 47– 51:

Jesus said: "Once again, the Kingdom of Heaven is like a net that was let down into the lake and caught all kinds of fish. When it was full, the fishermen pulled it up on the shore. Then they sat down and collected the good fish in baskets, but threw the bad away. This is how it will be at the end of the age. The angels will come and separate the wicked from the righteous and throw them into the fiery furnace, where there will be weeping and gnashing of teeth. Have you understood all these things?" Jesus asked. "Yes," they replied. (N.L.T.)

Granddad travelled from Peterchurch to Aberystwyth in order to find a fishing boat complete with a traditional type of net. Unfortunately, he soon discovered that the port of Aberystwyth was the centre of the Welsh lobster-fishing industry! There were few nets, but literally thousands of lobster pots! However, one very kind local fisherman found a 'Biblical' type of net and draped it over the stern of a fishing boat which was in the process of being renovated. As Granddad painted, a humorous story came into his mind about a Welsh 'fire and brimstone' preacher who was reminding his congregation about the ultimate perils of 'hell-fire and damnation'. "There will be weeping and gnashing of teeth", he remonstrated, his arms waving in the air.
An elderly member of the congregation, one Eli Jenkins, rose to his feet at the back of the Chapel.

"But, minister", he complained, "I ain't got any teeth!" The minister was quick to respond: "Teeth, Eli Jenkins," he said, "will be provided!"

When Granddad arrived home from his trip to west Wales, he proudly showed his picture of the Aberystwyth boat complete with fishing net, to Grandma.
"What do you think, darling?" he asked.
"There's one thing missing", Grandma replied.
"What's that?" came the innocent question.
"The fish, dear!"

After a stunned silence, Grandad got out his brushes, pens, and watercolours, and began to paint in the fish. He made them in different colours, shapes and sizes, leaving you to decide which ones are the 'good' fish, and which are the 'bad' ones. Again, I will end with Jesus' own words:

"Have you understood all these things?"

N is for Net

O is for the Owner of the Vineyard

Scripture Reference: Saint Luke Chapter 20 verses 9-10:

A man planted a vineyard, leased it out to tenant farmers, and moved to another country to live for several years. At grape-picking time, he sent one of his servants to collect his share of the crop. But the farmers attacked the servant, beat him up, and sent him back empty-handed. "What will I do?" the owner of the vineyard asked himself. "I know! I'll send my cherished son. Surely they will respect him."
(N.L.T.)

"Bill ~ will you pose for me as the 'Owner of the vineyard'? You can wear Kate's wide-brimmed straw hat, as protection from the sun, and you'll need a purple robe. Remember the French entrenching tool ~ the mattock? Perhaps you'd bring that as well? And, oh yes ~ one of your director's chairs to sit on. Perhaps you'd better wear that lovely pair of Roman leather sandals as well?"

Bill Greeves nodded in incredulous agreement, and we arranged to meet at 8am the following morning, in the adjacent vineyard, a few hundred yards down the road from 'le Pla', Joy and Bill's home in Caudies-de-Fenouillet. For Bill, the purple robe was no problem ~ he possessed a striking purple dust-sheet, which already had a convenient hole in the middle, for his head to pop through. And so it happened that Bill found himself sitting at the edge of a vineyard, authentically attired as a vineyard owner (circa A.D.30), wondering how long Bob would take to complete the painting. The heat was rising in direct proportion to the sun as it rose above the Pyrénées in the background. The face of the real owner of the vineyard, as he rounded the corner on his tractor was an incredible sight. I thought that it was only owls that could rotate their heads a full 360 degrees!

Children; the owner of the vineyard, the head of the estate, or the rich ruler in Jesus' parables is, of course, God the Father. God's purpose: to ensure that the fruitfulness of His produce is of the highest quality, and that it achieves its greatest yield. Have things ever changed in 2000 years? The vineyard is the Kingdom of Heaven. We are the grapes. Jesus is the vine; the Father is the husbandman, the owner of the vineyard. Fruitfulness? It's up to us!

Thank you, Bill, for bringing this tableau, this parable, to life.

O is for The Owner of the Vineyard

The Pearl of Great Price

Scripture Reference: Saint Matthew Chapter 13 verses 45–46:
Jesus said: "Again, the Kingdom of Heaven is like unto a merchant man, seeking goodly pearls; who, when he had found one pearl of great price, went and sold all that he had, and bought it." (A.V.)

Grandchildren, did you know that Jesus said: "Seek and ye shall find?"
It was not too difficult to find a fresh oyster in its shell, in the Champion Supermarket at St. Paul de Fenouillet. However, Grandad did feel rather like the merchant man, 'seeking goodly pearls', when he went in search of an imitation pearl to insert into the oyster shell so that he might have a 'living' example of a pearl of great price, waiting to be discovered in the fleshly folds of an oyster. As the oyster languished in our refrigerator, Grandma and Granddad continued their search for the elusive pearl. They had come to the conclusion that they did not need a 'pearl of great price' as such; rather, a pearl of very little price indeed, would suffice. At last, the discovery was made. They found a large imitation pearl in a gift shop belonging to a young couple who made jewellery, in a tiny mediaeval French village, late one Sunday afternoon. It was now time for Granddad to arrange his 'still life' composition! After cracking open the oyster with his trusty Swiss Army knife, Grandad placed the pearl in the now rather pungent corner of the oyster shell. The broken oyster was then placed on a blue serviette which was, in turn, placed on a pale maroon towel.

"Why don't you put some of the 'fruits of the spirit' into your painting of the pearl of great price?" came Grandma's helpful suggestion. And so it was that the inspired thoughts of 'she who must be obeyed', known to the family as the 'Anointed Oracle', became part of Granddad's mystical sea-fruit cocktail. Granddad obviously needs to dig himself out of trouble here, perhaps by letting Jesus have the last word:

"Lay not up for yourselves treasures upon earth, where moth and rust doth corrupt ... But lay up for yourselves treasures in heaven.
For where your treasure is, there will your heart be also."
Saint Matthew Chapter 6 verses 19-21 (Abridged from A.V.)

P is for the Pearl of Great Price

Q is for Quietness

Scripture Reference: Saint Luke Chapter 4 verses 42-43:

Early the next morning, Jesus went out into the wilderness. The crowds searched everywhere for Him, and when they finally found Him, they begged Him not to leave them. But He replied: "I must preach the good news of the Kingdom of God in other places too, because that is why I was sent." (N.L.T.)

Children; Grandma and Granddad were sitting outside 'le Grenier', a holiday home, on the patio built by Bill Greeves, within the confines of the original roof space of what was once a granary. Granddad was lying back in the sunlounger, looking at the brilliant azure-blue of the sky. Although there were no clouds to be seen in the sky, a variety of birds began to swoop and circle in the quietness of the evening atmosphere. Granddad wondered whether it would be possible to paint the unfathomable blue of the sky, and capture the quietness of the evening? As he began to paint, he followed the rhythms of the birds as they swooped and soared in the air-currents of the warm evening. The quietness was only disturbed by the rush of winged flight. No wonder Jesus sought the quietness of the wilderness in which to meditate and pray, he thought. Gradually, the picture began to take shape. Granddad's eyes, tired with looking continually into the impenetrable blue, began to suggest shapes and nuances which may not have been apparent to other observers. Each bird seemed to possess a different character, an alternative nature.

Granddad later learned, from a Vira resident, that he had painted a swift, a swallow, a house-marten, and three different species of insect-eating birds! Sometimes painting can be like prayer. You can be surprised with what comes into your mind. Jesus sought quietness so that He could pray, and be close to His Father. It is often good to seek quietness ~ to think, to pray, and to allow God to use our gifts and our abilities for His Kingdom.

Q is for Quietness

R is for Rainbow

Scripture Reference: Genesis Chapter 9 verses 12-13 and 16:

And God said, "This is the sign of the covenant I am making between me and you and every living creature with you, a covenant for all generations to come. I have set my rainbow in the clouds, and it will be the sign of the covenant between me and the earth. Whenever the rainbow appears in the clouds, I will see it and remember the everlasting covenant between God and all living creatures of every kind on the earth." (N.L.T.)

Children, the Rainbow is the heavenly sign of God's covenant love towards the masterpiece of His creation, the human person; and that means you and me. Throughout the ages, thinkers have attempted to define the awesome complexity of the Rainbow. However, definitions have resolutely remained in two distinct areas; the pragmatic and the spiritual.

Aristotle, the Greek philosopher, was probably the first pragmatist to attempt a 'scientific' definition. However, his admirable effort could be said to be flawed, because he believed the heavens to be finitely domed. His major contribution remains unaltered, in that he calculated that a human observer must fix their gaze at a certain angle, later acknowledged to be 42 degrees; in order to receive the image of the Rainbow through their eyes. The reason that a Rainbow defies the causal reasoning of the human person lies in the fact that, as a spiritual phenomenon, it contradicts the working of the pragmatic mind. Unlike a shadow or a cloud, which are also effects of atmosphere and light upon the human mind – and can be scientifically pinpointed in time and space – the Rainbow, insisting upon its role as the 'sign' of God's love towards the human observer – continues to defy the rules of the pragmatist, and the basic tenets of the scientist.

Why? Because, if you travel along a road, observing a Rainbow, the Rainbow will continue to travel with you, a constant reminder of God's covenant love. The shadow, the cloud, will remain where they were, obviously subject to the conditions of light and atmosphere which caused them. Thus, you may travel from Peterchurch to Clifford, and God's Rainbow will travel with you. You may share the beautiful colours with a friend or with a relative; red, orange, yellow, green, blue, indigo and violet. But, never forget that the Rainbow is, for your mind, and for your heart, the ultimate sign of God's covenant love.

R.S.MURRIN

R is for Rainbow

S is for Sower

Scripture Reference: Saint Matthew Chapter 13 verses 3 – 9:

Jesus said: " A farmer went out to sow his seed. As he was scattering the seed, some fell along the path, and the birds came and ate it up. Some fell on rocky places, where it did not have much soil. It sprang up quickly, because the soil was shallow. But when the sun came up, the plants were scorched, and they withered because they had no root. Other seed fell among thorns, which grew up and choked the plants. Still other seed fell on good soil, where it produced a crop – a hundred, sixty or thirty times what was sown. He who has ears, let him hear."
(N.L.T.)

Dear Grandchildren,

Jean Francois Millet (1814 - 1875) was a French painter who loved to paint the working men and women of France, during the nineteenth century. He was a man who studied his Bible, and whose faith always informed his work as an artist. Granddad knew, from his studies at Reading University School of Fine Art, that Millet had painted a superb oil painting of a French farmer sowing seeds by hand, in exactly the same way that Jesus had described in his parable. Granddad really struggled to find a reproduction of Millet's famous painting 'The Sower', until a lady from Church said that she would try to locate the elusive image on the Internet. The lady was successful, and Granddad went on one of his expeditions to Ty-Mawr Convent, near Monmouth, where, in their Print Room, sometimes used as an artist's studio, he painted his version of Millet's 'The Sower'. The parable of the sower is the central image of Jesus' teaching about the Kingdom of Heaven. Thankfully, children, if you read further into Chapter 13 of Matthew's Gospel, you will find the meaning of the parable, in Jesus' own words:

"But the one who received the seed that fell on good soil is the one who hears the word and understands it." (Verse 23)

There's an old English saying, "You reap what you sow." Simply,
it means that if you sow bad seed all your life, the result will be a bad harvest. But, if you continually sow good seed, as the farmer in the picture, striding through his fields at the dawn of the day is doing, you will reap a wonderful harvest of good things; and then,

The Kingdom of Heaven will be yours.

S is for the Sower

T is for Treasure

Scripture reference: St.Matthew Chapter 13 verse 44:

Jesus said "The Kingdom of Heaven is like a treasure that a man discovered hidden in a field. In his excitement, he hid it again and sold everything he owned to get enough money to buy the field ~ and to get the treasure too!" (N.L.T.)

It was the hottest day of the year so far; not only in Vira, but throughout southern France. Grandma and Granddad later learned that the temperatures in our area had risen to 41.6 degrees centigrade! We are told that 'mad dogs and Englishmen go out in the midday sun!' Granddad must have been mad to venture out with his chair, his cushion, and his painting equipment on that particular day, having already prepared 'the Treasure' which he was intending to paint. The treasure was comprised of a Greek-style earthenware pot, Grandma's imitation gold necklace, and a handful of gold, silver, and bronze Euro coins from Granddad's pocket!

With the French entrenching tool, or mattock, over his shoulder, Granddad ventured out in the sweltering heat to find a shady corner of a vineyard, where he could arrange the 'still-life' composition which would depict the freshly discovered Treasure in Jesus' parable. Perspiring profusely, Granddad scrabbled in the loose earth in the corner of the vineyard, and arranged the mattock, the earthenware pot, and the Treasure. Perfection! Granddad lost no time in positioning his chair, and began to paint. What made the composition even more interesting, was the background of French lavender flowers, proudly adding their beauty to the arrangement.

It was while painting the more intricate details of the stones and coins that Granddad first noticed that some very large, dark brown ants were parading up and down his leg, in precise military formation. What Granddad did not realise, was that he had plonked one of the legs of his chair right in the centre of an ant's nest! Horrified, Granddad stood bolt upright, failing to stop his pad, his paints, and his water container from tumbling to the ground. It seemed as if the painting was going nowhere. However, as Granddad settled back down, trying to bring new life into the picture of this freshly discovered treasure; things got better and better, and the painting was soon finished, ready for you to appreciate. Children, I hope that you will discover the secret of the Kingdom of Heaven in Granddad's watercolour of 'T is for Treasure.'

T is for Treasure

U is for the Unjust Judge

Scripture reference: Saint Luke Chapter 18 verses 2-7:

Jesus said "In a certain town there was a judge who neither feared God nor cared about men. And there was a widow in that town who kept coming to him with the plea: 'Grant me justice against my adversary.' For some time he refused. But finally he said to himself, 'Even though I don't fear God or care about men, yet because this widow keeps bothering me, I will see that she gets justice, so that she won't eventually wear me out with her coming!' And the Lord said, 'Listen to what the unjust judge says. And will not God bring about justice for his chosen ones, who cry out to him day and night? Will he keep putting them off? I tell you, he will see that they get justice, and quickly. However, when the Son of Man comes, will he find faith on the earth?" (N.L.T.)

Kiddiewinkies; a frightening wind was howling around 'le Grenier,' a converted barn high in the French Pyrénées. The shutters rattled, and it seemed as if the patter of heavy reptilian feet would eventually bring the roof crashing down on a very restless Granddad and Grandma. Unknown to us we were experiencing the infamous 'Trans-Montaigne Blast', which roars around the Pyrénées on various occasions, lasting for as little as twenty-four hours, or for as long as a week. As Granddad lay awake, his thoughts turned once again to the 'A-Z of the Kingdom of Heaven.' What on earth, or in heaven would the letter 'U' stand for? And then, the image of an unjust judge came to mind. In fact, the image did not just come to mind, it was more like a three-dimensional picture of an incredibly large judge, whose main characteristics were meanness, avarice, haughtiness, and lack of humanity. Not only did the technicolour image arrive, uninvited, in the theatre of my subconscious mind, but it was accompanied by a tune, the judge's song, straight from the musical score of Gilbert and Sullivan's 'Trial by Jury':

"When I, dear friends, was called to the bar, I'd an appetite hale and hearty,
For I was as many young barristers are, an impecunious party.
I'd a swallow-tail coat of a beautiful hue,
And a brief that I'd bought off a booby,
A couple of shirts, and a collar or two,
And a ring that looked like a ruby!"

My unjust judge, and the judge from 'Trial by Jury' have a lot in common. They both share one important characteristic, they are unjust! The morning after our night of interrupted sleep, Grandma and I settled down to our respective pastimes. Grandma read her book, but I still had the magnificent image of the unjust judge in my mind. The image translated itself onto my artist's paper with delightful, colourful ease. Even the judge's desk seemed appropriate for him, with his quill pen, and his gavel, poised to deliver his verdict. Children, I hope you like my picture of the unjust judge. Can you see the diminutive figure of the widow in the bottom right hand corner of the composition? If, like her, you are persistent in your prayers, then the Good Lord will certainly grant your requests.

U is for the Unjust Judge

V is for Vine

Scripture Reference: Saint John Chapter 15 verses 1–5a:

Jesus said, "I am the true vine, and my Father is the gardener.
He cuts off every branch in me that bears no fruit, while every branch
that does bear fruit He prunes so that it will be even more fruitful.
You are already clean because of the word I have spoken to you.
Remain in me, and I will remain in you. No branch can bear fruit by
itself; it must remain in the vine. Neither can you bear fruit unless you
remain in me. I am the vine; you are the branches. If a person remains
in me and I in them, they will bear much fruit." (N.L.T.)

Little treasures; Granddad could hardly wait to get to the village of Vira, in
the Pyrénees, in the late September of 2002. He knew that the 'fields would
be ripe unto harvest', and that there would be clusters of grapes for him to
feature in his painting book, hanging from the vines in the many vineyards
dotted around the area. The late summer sun had brought the fruit to full
ripeness, and Granddad and Grandma could often see the pickers in the
fields, beginning to gather in the harvest. The village of Vira itself was no
exception, and you could see the bunches of grapes belonging to Monsieur
Henri Dimond, hanging in their deep purple clusters on the vines just below
our balcony. Granddad borrowed a chair, and with his battered Cézanne hat
on his head, went down on the first morning of his holiday, to paint the
variety of grape known as 'le Cardinal' on Monsieur Dimond's vines.

What an incredible image Jesus paints with his words, "I am the true vine."
Jesus is telling us that we can only be fruitful if we are rooted deeply in Him.
If we take the imagery to its logical conclusion, then, there must be a harvest
time when we will be crushed, like the grapes growing in the Languedoc-
Roussilon area of France, in order to make the season's new wine. Will we
make a sour, vinegary wine, distasteful to God's palate? Or, will we
experience the privilege of being turned into a vintage wine, sweet to the
Lord's tongue, and of nutritious value to the Kingdom of Heaven? Children,
Jesus wants you to be fruitful, like the grapes on Monsieur Dimond's vines,
because, as Jesus says:

"This is to my Father's glory, that you bear much fruit,
showing yourselves to be my disciples!"

V is for Vine

W is for the Wheat and the Tares

Scripture Reference: Saint Matthew Chapter 13 verses 24-26:

Jesus said "The Kingdom of Heaven is likened unto a man which sowed good seed in his field. But while people slept, his enemy came and sowed tares among the wheat, and went his way. But when the blade was sprung up, and brought forth fruit, then appeared the tares also." (A.V.)

"I'm looking for a field of wheat, preferably with some thistles in the foreground," said Granddad to Grandma, during their holiday in Vira, in June 2003. "Perhaps they don't grow wheat in this part of France," was Grandma's somewhat unhelpful reply. "Well, I'm going to keep on looking," Granddad said, even though seeds of doubt had been sown in his mind by Grandma's less than encouraging conclusion. Granddad scoured the fields and hedgerows around Vira for the elusive sheaves of wheat, finding many more thistles than ears of corn or maize. Eventually, Granddad settled for a cluster of plants, looking like miniature versions of 'corn-on-the-cob', because they had a strong, vibrant, sea-green thistle growing immediately in front of them, and because this eminently suitable subject was only a few yards from their comfortable holiday home, The converted barn, so sensitively designed by Bill and Joy Greeves.

Jesus loved the countryside! He knew that his listeners would understand stories about vineyards, flocks of sheep, fig trees, and fields of wheat ~ and, yes, those maddening things which were the bane of every countryperson ~ weeds! What could be worse than a field of waving wheat, interspersed with dark green, thorny, virulent weeds? There was one thing worse, and that was when those weeds had been planted by an enemy. In the parable of the Wheat and the Tares, the wheat has, in fact, been planted by an enemy. The workers expect the farmer to give the order: 'Root them out!' However, they are somewhat surprised to hear the instructions to allow the weeds to grow with the wheat until harvest-time. It is at the harvest that they will be rooted out, and burned. It is the same with our spiritual lives. Sometimes we have to live with irritations and imperfections; often, with false accusations aimed at us from other people. At the harvest, our goodness and fruitfulness will be rewarded, and the weeds of negativity and doubt will disappear for ever.

W is for the Wheat and the Tares

X IS FOR IXTHUS

IXTHUS (THE FISH) ~ AN EARLY CRYPTOGRAM SIGNIFYING
THE CHRISTIAN FAITH: IESU XRISTOS THEO UIOUS SOTERIOS
JESUS CHRIST ~ SON OF GOD ~ SAVIOUR

SCRIPTURE REFERENCE: SAINT JOHN CHAPTER 6 VERSES 8-9:

ANOTHER OF HIS DISCIPLES, ANDREW, SIMON PETER'S BROTHER, SAID
TO HIM: "THERE IS A LITTLE BOY HERE, WHO HAS WITH HIM FIVE BARLEY
LOAVES AND TWO FISH. BUT WHAT GOOD IS THAT WITH THIS HUGE
CROWD?" (N.L.T.)

CHILDREN, I LOVE THE PICTURE OF THE FISH! DON'T YOU? THE TWO
MACKEREL ARE SUCH GREAT CHARACTERS, AND WHAT A PITY IT IS THAT
THEY WERE EATEN BY GRANDMA AND GRANDDAD, WHEN GRANDDAD HAD
FINISHED PAINTING THEM. I DON'T KNOW WHETHER GRANDDAD TOOK
TOO LONG PAINTING THE TWO FISH, BUT HE CERTAINLY HAD AN UPSET
STOMACH THROUGHOUT THE NIGHT, AND WELL INTO THE NEXT DAY.

THE WORD 'IXTHUS' MEANS 'FISH' IN THE GREEK LANGUAGE, AND IT
WAS A WORD USED BY THE VERY EARLY CHRISTIANS, WHO, LIVING UNDER
PERSECUTION, OFTEN USED SECRET SIGNS AND SYMBOLS TO
COMMUNICATE WITH EACH OTHER. TODAY, YOU CAN USUALLY TELL THAT
IT IS A CHRISTIAN WHO IS DRIVING THE CAR IN FRONT OF YOU, BECAUSE
OF THE LITTLE METAL FISH SYMBOL ATTACHED TO THE BACK OF THEIR
VEHICLE.

WHEN I WAS A YOUNG MAN, I USED TO GO OUT WITH MY GRANDFATHER,
WHO OWNED A STURDILY BUILT WOODEN MOTOR BOAT, MOORED IN THE
CREEK AT KINGSWEAR, ON THE RIVER DART. WE USED TO VENTURE OUT
TOGETHER, TOWARDS THE MOUTH OF THE RIVER, OFTEN THROUGH VERY
CHOPPY WATER, WITH MACKEREL-SPINNING LINES TRAILING BEHIND US.
WHAT FUN IT WAS WHEN A MACKEREL TOOK THE BAIT, AND YOU COULD
HAUL IN A SHIMMERING, SILVER-STREAKED FISH, PLACING YOUR CATCH
WELL INTO THE CENTRE OF THE BOAT, ADMIRING THE MULTI-COLOURED
RAINBOW FACETS OF ITS COAT.

THE TWO MACKEREL PURCHASED AT THE FISH COUNTER AT THE
CHAMPION SUPERMARKET IN SAINT PAUL DE FENOUILLET WERE
SIMILARLY HANDSOME. IT WAS LEFT TO ME TO IMAGINE THE LETTERS
'I-X-T-H-U-S' WITHIN THE MULTI-COLOURED SCALES OF THE SMALLER FISH.
IT WAS ALMOST AS IF THE 'WORD' WAS ALREADY THERE, SUBTLY HIDDEN,
MILLIMETRES UNDER THE HARDENING SCALES OF THE FISH'S SIDE. WHAT
AN AMAZING THING IT IS TO REALISE THAT THE CHRISTIAN SYMBOL OF THE
FISH HAS REMAINED WITH US FOR CENTURIES. LET US HOPE THAT
WHENEVER WE COME ACROSS A FISH, IN WHATEVER CIRCUMSTANCES,
OUR HEARTS WILL LEAP WITH JOY AS WE REMEMBER THE IDIOM:

"JESUS CHRIST ~ SON OF GOD ~ SAVIOUR."

R.S.MURRN

X IS FOR IXTHUS

Y is for Yeast

Scripture references: Saint Matthew Chapter 13 verse 33, and Chapter 16 verses 6 and 11-12.

Jesus also used this illustration: "The Kingdom of Heaven is like yeast used by a woman making bread. Even though she used a large amount of flour, the yeast permeated every part of the dough." ..."Watch out!" Jesus warned them. "Beware of the yeast of the Pharisees and Sadducees ... How could you ever think I was talking about food? So, again I say: Beware of the yeast of the Pharisees and Sadducees." Then, at last, they understood that He wasn't speaking about yeast or bread, but about the false teaching of the Pharisees and Sadducees. (N.L.T.)

Don't you know, children, that Grandma doesn't normally make bread. In fact, I could say that Grandma hasn't made any bread for a very long time. If I say any more, I'll definitely be in trouble! Thankfully, the Supermarket in Saint Paul de Fenouillet had one packet of French country-style, "Bake-it-at-home bread" left on the shelves. Reluctantly, Grandma added the liquid to the powder as Granddad prepared his paints. I could tell from the look in Grandma's eyes that she was not going to give me very much time to complete my painting. As I painted, much faster than I normally paint, the bread mixture became more stodgy, and far more sticky. In fact, Grandma could not extricate her fingers from the light-brown quagmire which was about to overflow from the mixing bowl. "Hurry up, Bob," she pleaded, as I drew and painted like Jackson Pollock, the American artist who loved to splash paint onto his canvases; having a brainstorm. "I'll have to put it to one side now," Kate concluded, "to allow the yeast to do its work."

I continued to paint, my model having retired to scrape the remaining dough off her hands. I know that the yeast permeated every part of the dough, because the bread, when it came out of the oven, was the finest tasting country-style bread that you could ever wish to taste. If we allow the Kingdom of Heaven to become the yeast in the workings of our lives; then, Jesus promises us an excellent result - just like Grandma's perfect country-style bread!

Y is for Yeast

Z IS FOR ZOE
(ZOE IS A WONDERFUL GREEK WORD MEANING 'LIFE')

SCRIPTURE REFERENCES: SAINT JOHN CHAPTER 10
VERSE 10, AND CHAPTER 12 VERSE 25:
JESUS ANSWERED: "I AM COME THAT THEY MIGHT HAVE LIFE,
AND HAVE IT MORE ABUNDANTLY... HE THAT LOVETH HIS LIFE
SHALL LOSE IT: AND HE THAT HATETH HIS LIFE
IN THIS WORLD SHALL KEEP IT UNTO LIFE ETERNAL." (A.V.)

CHILDREN, HAVE YOU EVER TRIED TO PAINT A BUTTERFLY? GRANDDAD TRIED FOR A WHOLE MORNING, JUST OUTSIDE THE VILLAGE OF VIRA, ONE VERY HOT DAY IN EARLY JUNE, 2003. THE PYRÉNEAN BUTTERFLIES (THEY WERE MANY AND INCREDIBLY BEAUTIFUL) EITHER CLOSED THEIR GOSSAMER WINGS RESOLUTELY, OR FLITTED OFF TO PASTURES NEW. GRANDDAD EVENTUALLY GAVE UP, AND RETURNED HOME TO THE BARN CONVERSION, 'LE GRENIER', "TIRED AND EMOTIONAL" (A PHRASE USED BY THE LATE LORD GEORGE BROWN, AS AN EXCUSE WHEN HE FAILED TO FIND HIS FOOTING AFTER A NIGHT OUT). GRANDMA, HAVING COLLAPSED DISCONSOLATELY ON THE SOFA, ADVISED GRANDDAD: "WELL, YOU CAN ALWAYS PAINT A BUTTERFLY STRAIGHT FROM YOUR IMAGINATION!" (WHICH IS WHAT HE DID!)

THE GREEK WORD FOR LIFE, ZOE, IS HEAVY WITH MEANING. ANCIENT GREEK WRITERS SUCH AS HOMER, USED ZOE TO PORTRAY THE CREATIVITY OF LIFE, OR THE PROCREATIVE CAPABILITIES WITHIN LIFE ITSELF. ONE SUCH WRITER WONDERED HOW A SCULPTOR, ENGAGED UPON A STONE CARVING, MIGHT BE ABLE TO BRING THAT PARTICULAR WORK OF ART TO LIFE? JESUS, HOWEVER, IN CHAPTER 10 OF SAINT JOHN'S GOSPEL, GETS TO THE HEART OF THE MATTER BY ANNOUNCING THAT HE HAS COME IN ORDER TO BRING ABUNDANT LIFE TO THOSE WHO BELIEVE IN HIM. ZOE, HOWEVER, IS NOT THE SHADOW OF LIFE WHICH MAY, OR MAY NOT BE PERCEIVED IN A STONE STATUE. RATHER, IT IS THE ABUNDANT, TRANSCENDENT LIFE PROMISED TO THOSE WHO SEE, AND BELIEVE IN THE KINGDOM OF HEAVEN. MY VERY BRIGHT WATERCOLOUR SHOWS A PYRÉNEAN BUTTERFLY, EMERGING FROM ITS CHRYSALIS, FULL OF THE GENEROUS, CREATIVE, ABUNDANT AND TRANSCENDENT LIFE SPOKEN ABOUT BY JESUS. THE THEME OF ZOE, LIFE, OCCURS AGAIN AND AGAIN THROUGHOUT SAINT JOHN'S GOSPEL. IN CHAPTER 12, JESUS URGES US TO LAY DOWN, OR GIVE UP OUR MORTAL, DECAYING, EGO-CENTRIC LIVES, AND GRASP THE PROMISES WHICH ZOE LIFE GIVES. JESUS WANTS ALL OF US TO EXPERIENCE THE ABUNDANCE, THE GENEROSITY, THE TRANSCENDENCE OF THIS ZOE LIFE. IF WE BELIEVE IN HIM, LAYING DOWN THE BROKEN CHRYSALIS OF OUR SINFUL LIVES, WE HAVE THE PROMISE OF THAT OTHER DIMENSION WHICH ZOE OFFERS ~

ETERNAL LIFE!

Z is for Zoe

BRITISH COPYRIGHT LAW
